JOURNEYS AND STORIES

PORTO

AND NORTHERN PORTUGAL

A JOURNEY THROUGH NORTHERN PORTUGAL

PEDRO VELOSO / SUSANA FONSECA / SÉRGIO FONSECA

A discussão
de

Introduction

A country is born, it becomes a nation, flourishes, gains an identity and memories. Portugal was born in the North.

History is constructed in the fortified villages, the Roman roads, the medieval churches, the ancient manor houses and in each stone remaining of the castles. The origins of our people are linked to the city of Guimarães and to the bravery of our first King, D. Afonso Henriques, who went southwards, conquering land from the Moors.

In Northern Portugal, cultural richness and natural beauty are unique and diverse.

At the heart of Minho are tales of brave women. The coastline, along the blue Atlantic, is rich in salt, seaweed and legends about fishing and the sea.

The hills share their space with the granite and the green of the forests, where leafy trees, such as oak and beech, predominate, forming parks of singular beauty, like Peneda Gerês.

In lands of beliefs, religion is essential for the faithful, and there are many constructions devoted to God. The city of Braga is an example of religious experience.

Granite is one of the symbols of the North, and its touch, rough and hard, resembles the hands of its people, hands of labour and hard work. This representation is mirrored in the streets and façades of Porto, Guimarães or Ponte de Lima, where the people counter the austerity of the stone with smiles that light up the ways.

Porto is a city of bridges. To cross them is to travel in time. It is to begin a journey of memories from the Rabelo boats to the balconies of the Ribeira houses. Porto is an open house welcoming those who are well-intentioned. It is an invitation to discover the Port Wine route and the terraces of the Douro.

Gastronomy is vast and varied, one of the attractions of this region. From the fish dishes, typical of the coastline areas, to game dishes in the mountain regions, the choice offers great quality.

To travel through the North is to say, "Here I felt, smiled, loved and prayed". It is to say that I allowed myself to be taken down memory lane and wish I had stayed.

Pedro Rodrigues

01

02

The present city of **Porto**, as a community aggregator, with its different social facets, started more than 100 000 years ago, with small groups of hunter-gatherers, mainly spread along the coastline. The growing dominance of agriculture and grazing led to the emergence of the first settlements, which strongly thrived with metallurgical exploitation from the 4th millennium BC.

Later, in 1123, bishop D. Hugo granted the charter to the city's inhabitants, which boosted the settlement and development of the town.

In the late Middle Ages, Porto consisted of a walled episcopal area, and became the meeting point of routes and the link with other regions. The Cathedral Hill and the Ribeira were probably the most populated areas. It was inside the walls of this city that, in 1387, King D. João I married Philippa of Lancaster, in order to strengthen the Anglo-Portuguese Alliance. Born of this marriage, and probably in Porto, was Prince Henry the Navigator, a great driver of the Discoveries.

Still connected with this period, tradition registers that the city's population gave away all the meat to feed the men who took part in the expedition that Prince Henry led to Ceuta, during 1415. The people were left with the offal for their own sustenance, which gave rise to the famous gastronomic dish called "Tripas à Moda do Porto" (Porto-style tripe).

The city's mercantile influence spread to the various neighbouring settlements over the centuries, and the River Douro was a prime route for the transport of goods, including the famous Port Wine.

For that reason, too, Porto was one of the cities that most suffered during the Peninsular Wars. People still talk of the terrible catastrophe of 29 March 1809, when a large number of people who were fleeing from and being chased by the French, drowned in their beloved River Douro, caused by the collapse of the fragile barge bridge. Porto's inhabitants played a key role in defending liberal ideals, offering their city as headquarters for the Liberal Revolution, in 1820, and ensuring the success of the movement when they stoically withstood a hard siege, by the troops of D. Miguel I in 1832. Due to the courage with which the inhabitants resisted the siege, Queen D. Maria II gave the city the name "Invicta Cidade

Engraving with a view of Serra do Pilar during the Siege of Porto (Porto Municipal Historical Archive)

do Porto" – "Unvanquished City of Porto" - unique among the other cities.

The dogged defence of principles such as democracy, equality and humanism, was once again revealed at the end of the 19th century, with the first important demonstration to establish the Republic and overthrow the monarchy, on 31 January 1891.

More recently, Porto once again showed itself to the world, when it was designated 2001 European Culture Capital, extending new dynamics and cultural events of great prominence throughout its urban fabric, also marking its landscape with new infrastructures, Casa da Música being the most emblematic.

Whilst Porto, through its old toponym - *Portus Cale* - gave the country its name, its people have, since remote times, always honoured commitments within the regional and national scope, contributing to the flourishing of a great nation, built with great efforts, courage, adventure and science, all originating in a small territory.

Casa do Infante, so named for the fact that Henry the Navigator was born there, is located in the historical centre of Porto. This building now houses the Municipal Historical Archive, where the majority of this information can be confirmed in its vast collection of documentation.

The building also houses a Museum, where visitors may see traces of the Roman, Medieval and Early Modern occupation of the city, with particular emphasis on the former Royal Customs House and the Mint.

←

01- Front of the Charter granted to the city of Porto by

D. Manuel I in 1517 (Porto Municipal Historical Archive)

02- Henry the Navigator

Image of the suspension bridge over the Douro (Porto Municipal Historical Archive)

D. Luís I bridge seen from the viewpoint at Serra do Pilar

Ribeira do Porto, photo of the collection of the Instituto dos Vinhos do Douro e do Porto

During the first half of the 19th century, Porto suffered several situations of political instability such as the Peninsular War and the Liberal Wars, which culminated with the **Siege of Porto** (1832-1833), leaving signs of destruction all over town.

During the siege, the liberal troops of D. Pedro were besieged by the royalist forces of D. Miguel, with a disproportion of more than 8 000 soldiers under siege to 80 000 besiegers. The heroic resistance of the liberal troops and of the population of Porto had ended with a victory, despite the hard conditions and despair resulting from constant attacks, hunger and epidemics. Therefore, Porto earned the title of *Civitas Invicta* – Unvanquished City.

The second half of the century brought great dynamism to the city, consequently resulting in a population increase and a reorganisation of the urban structure. To cross the River Douro several bridges were built over time, starting with the Barge Bridge, then the Suspension Bridge, Maria Pia Bridge (railway) and D. Luís I Bridge.

The **Suspension Bridge** was in operation for about 45 years. Today one can still see what is left of the pillars of this bridge, near D. Luís I Bridge.

Porto Crystal Palace, 1901/1951

São Bento Railway Station, 1896

Avenida dos Aliados, 1920/1950

Clérigos' Tower, 1920/1950

Porto Town Hall, 1960/1964

The **Cathedral** is one of the most relevant monuments of the city. It is located in the heart of the historical centre and rises in the landscape as an eye-catching icon, welcoming visitors. Historic testimonies point to the existence of a previous, simpler religious construction, on the site of the current temple. The start of the Cathedral's construction, in the Romanesque style, dates back to the 12th century. At that time, the episcopal town was organised around the cathedral.

Surrounding it were streets, narrow lanes, small squares and alleys. In 1387, the Cathedral was embellished to celebrate the wedding of King D. João I with the English princess Philippa of Lancaster (reinforcing the Anglo-Portuguese Alliance). On the North tower there is a bas-relief which represents a boat from the 14th century (a "coca"), symbolizing the maritime vocation of the city. The exterior underwent significant alterations in the Baroque and Gothic periods. Inside, note the sacristy, the cloister and the silver altar of the Blessed Sacrament.

↑ *Cathedral and Pillory*
→ *(from top to right)*
01- Cathedral Nave
02- Silver Altar
03- Altar of Nossa Senhora da Silva
04- High Altar

Guindais Steps

Muralha Fernandina

Muralha Fernandina is the name given to the system of walls that protected the city of Porto, parts of which are still visible today, namely the well preserved stretch along the escarpment parallel to Guindais funicular; the Ribeira Wall which continues to Bacalhoeiros Wall by the river; the section of the building of the former English Club in Rua das Virtudes, and remaining segments integrated in the houses on Rua Dr. Barbosa de Castro and Rua das Taipas.

This defensive structure was restored over the ages, up to the recent period of the New State.

During the 14th century, Porto expanded beyond the initial borough, which was located around the Cathedral, surrounded by an earlier defensive Romanesque wall, a legacy of Roman engineering. Increased trading and maritime activities led to the need to build a wider fortified enclosure to protect the burghers and their business premises, located in the riverside area. For many years, access through Guindais connected the two urban centres and, in a certain way, gave some sense of order to the layout of the new walls, whose construction was ordered by D. Afonso IV, although they were only concluded during the reign of King D. Fernando, hence the name 'Muralha Fernandina'.

The 13th century represented an expansion period for the city of Porto. At that time, there were already two settlement areas: one in the high town, around the Cathedral, and another down below, in *Ribeira*, near the River Douro. The urban fabric grew due to the connection between these two areas, increasing the accesses and communications between them, framing new housing and public areas with the proliferation of houses, streets, steps and lanes, such as *Rua da Lada*, *Rua da Reboleira* and *Rua dos Banhos*.

The oldest axis connecting the two agglomerations continued through *Rua de D. Hugo* and the *Escadas do Barredo*.

Later, another axis with better accessibility was opened, formed by *Rua dos Mercadores*, *Rua da Bainharia* and *Rua Escura*.

Nowadays, as you walk these routes, either in Ribeira, or up the streets leading to the Cathedral you will live and feel Porto's history.

At *Rua da Reboleira* you will find examples of architecture from the end of the Middle Ages (14th century). The original structure of the tower house at nº 59 is still intact.

← *Ribeira do Porto*

→ *(from top to right)*

01- Travessa do Barredo

02- Rua da Reboleira

03- Rua da Fonte Taurina

04- Rua dos Mercadores

Illustrated Ribeira

The façades of the colourful houses line the streets, displaying their elegance in full sight of the sweet and beloved River Douro. It is the tale of a platonic love with no end in sight, and so each house adopts its own adornment with clothes on the balcony or flowerpots in the windows, impressing those who pass.

These façades, accompanied by their beloved river, the narrow lanes bearing the marks of time, the majestic Clérigos Tower and the Rabelo boats are part of this unique place, captured by the lenses of the tourists.
I know of what I speak for I have often witnessed admiring glances being exchanged and heard flattering phrases in many languages of the world. I myself feel special to be part of this space, belonging to mankind. I know also that one day it will be my turn to leave and by then my duty will be done for I will take with me a piece of this city, made of mists and smiles.

Ever since I was brought here, every single morning I am placed outside, within view of the visitors. During the night I rest in a dark shop surrounded by objects that show the city photographed, illustrated, magnetised, embroidered, carved and even spiritualised. Whilst I repose, I think how much I will miss the authentic warmth of the population, who welcome people with smiles of gold and gruff voices. Even so, I am prepared to be removed quite soon from the postcard display and be sent, with a message, to a distant place, where I will continue to display the façades of my colourful and aligned houses, eternally in love with a golden river.

Susana Fonseca

↑ ↓ ↘ *Photos from the collection of the Instituto dos Vinhos do Douro e do Porto*

Port Wine is produced from grapes cultivated in the Douro Demarcated Region, a World Heritage Site, located about 100 km from Porto.

Although produced with grapes from the Douro and stored in the lodges in Vila Nova de Gaia, this drink became known as "Port Wine" from the second half of the 17th century, as it was exported from this town to the four corners of the world.

One of the characteristics which make Port Wine different to other wines is the fact that its fermentation is not finished, due to the addition of a neutral grape spirit. Port is a naturally sweet wine, stronger than other wines.

← *pages 18 / 19, Ribeira do Porto*

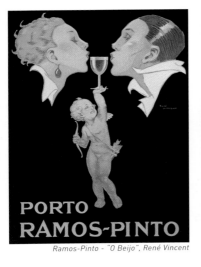

Ramos-Pinto - "O Beijo", René Vincent

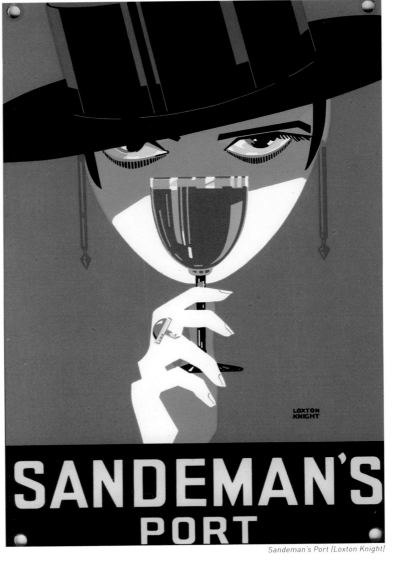

Sandeman's Port (Loxton Knight)

Corrêa Ribeiro & Filhos (Monte Carlo)

Rabelo is a Portuguese boat, typical of River Douro, which traditionally transported the oak casks with Port Wine from Upper Douro to Vila Nova de Gaia, where the wine was stored, aged, bottled and sold.

The traditional *Rabelo* boat has 748 to 905 inches long. Its construction type, named Clinter Built, is a perfect symbiosis of the Nordic, Mediterranean and Oriental techniques, which adapt to a very particular river and activities. The boat was manned by 6 or 7 men, who used a long paddle at the stern to guide it.

With the arrival of the hydroelectric exploitation of the river, the *Rabelos* were no longer used since 1961. Nowadays they are a tourist attraction of River Douro, especially when taking part of the famous regatta of *São João*.

↑ Rabelo boats

↑ Regatta of Rabelo boats

→ Rabelo boat at the beginning of the
20th century, photo from the collection of the
Instituto dos Vinhos do Douro e do Porto

Houses at Praça da Ribeira

Ribeira is one of Porto's most ancient and attractive places. It is located next to the River Douro and is part of the city's historical centre, classified as a World Heritage Site by UNESCO. It is known that since the 12th century this area expanded with the construction of houses and steps and with new streets and lanes being opened.

The major development during the 14th century meant the rise in importance of all maritime and commercial activities.

At the beginning of the 15th century Ribeira used to be crowded with people connected to the river and the sea, it was a world of merchants and gave rise to the middle-class, with its centre in Praça da Ribeira.

Nowadays it is an area much visited by tourists, with many bars, esplanades, restaurants and handicraft shops. The houses in Ribeira form a unique ensemble, illustrated on the city's postcards and relived in the eyes of its visitors.

← "O Cubo", by José Rodrigues at Praça da Ribeira

→ (from top to bottom)

01/02- Houses at Ribeira near Cais da Estiva

Aerial view over Porto and the River Douro

São João Bridge

Freixo Bridge

D. Maria Pia Bridge

S. João Bridge is a railway bridge designed by the engineer Edgar Cardoso and built between 1984 and 1991. Its project, with a central span of 250 metres, set a world record for this type of bridge.

Freixo Bridge was designed by Professor António Reis. It is composed of two twin beams set 10 cm apart all along the way. It is located upriver of all the other bridges.

Infante Bridge was inaugurated in 2003 under the responsibility of the engineer Adão da Fonseca. The bridge is 371 metres long and its deck 20 metres wide. In view of its dimensions and typology it was considered one of the world's most elegant bridges.

Arrábida Bridge was built between 1956 and 1963, and was the first bridge over the Douro to be made entirely with Portuguese engineering. The respected engineer Edgar Cardoso planned this bridge, which was considered one of the world's longest arch bridges made of reinforced concrete. It was a work of bold and original engineering which attracted several foreign technical experts and journalists. Nowadays it is still used for road and pedestrian traffic.

Arrábida Bridge

Infante Bridge

D. Maria Pia Bridge was built in 1887, by Eiffel et Cie. It has been considered a National Monument since 1982 and for seven years held the world record of the longest span, as its deck which is 353 metres long, lies on one single arch at a height of 61 metres above the river. D. Maria Pia Bridge was a work built "at the limit of the classic possibilities of iron construction", according to the words spoken more than 100 years ago by the French engineer Eiffel, whose names graces the famous tower in Paris. The bridge was part of the Porto-Lisbon railway connection for many years. It was decommissioned in 1991 and replaced by S. João Bridge.

D. Luís I Bridge was built over the River Douro to replace the Suspension Bridge, and was constructed by the Belgian company Societé de Willebroeck, following a design by the engineer Téophile Seyrig. It was inaugurated in 1886 and classified as a National Monument in 1982. It has one of the world's largest wrought iron arches and two decks.

Nowadays the upper deck is used by one of Porto Metro lines, and the lower deck, measuring 174 metres long, offers one way of reaching Vila Nova de Gaia, whether by car or on foot.

→ *pages 30 / 31, D. Luís I bridge seen from the viewpoint at Serra do Pilar*

Felgueiras Lighthouse

"Homem do Leme", by Américo Gomes

In the 16th century, **Foz Velha**, located on the western edge of the city, was a fishing and rural settlement. The importance of this settlement involved the military defence of the entrance to the Douro Bar, hence the existence of the "Castelo do Queijo" and "São João da Foz" forts.

This situation has changed since the mid-19th century, when elegant neighbourhoods were built, and the houses were occupied by several British families to indulge in the fashion for sea bathing. Coffee shops, hotels, gambling houses and the famous baths lent Foz a cosmopolitan atmosphere, enhanced by the rising number of holidaymakers.

Nowadays, the beach zone is busy throughout the year, and enlivened by bars, esplanades and restaurants. The seaside promenade, enjoyed by pedestrians and cyclists, is privileged by the beauty of nature. "Pérgola da Foz", a romantic viewpoint, and the statue of the "Homem do Leme" – The Helmsman, are part of this sophisticated environment, which is enjoyed by visitors.

Pérgola da Foz

Cais da Lingueta

Fort of São Francisco de Xavier (Castelo do Queijo)

Passeio Alegre

Passage along the banks of the River Douro

Avenida dos Aliados

I went up towards the Town Hall. The sky rumbled and opened onto Porto, unleashing laments that included steady rainfall. One could barely distinguish the white pedestrian crossings under the downpour that shook my poor umbrella, already twisted by other storms.

As soon as I reached the door of Guarany Café, I walked in on an impulse, leaving trails of water wherever I passed. Thus I remained for a few moments, drenched and momentarily wretched. As if by magic a cup of hot coffee eased my discomfort. I watched the storm and the dark morning. I remembered the story a friend had told me about an Englishman who had lived in Porto in the 18th century. He is believed to have been responsible for supervising and executing several urban works in the city, but people also considered that he had made a pact with the devil, for he was able to attract the grey lightning-bearing clouds to his gardens. No doubt, today would have been a perfect day for his experiments with the lightning conductor, which certainly involved science rather than witchcraft. What would he think of this avenue that he never knew? This avenue which welcomes the rain and the sun with the same generosity? All these cars, which pass by taking people to their destinations, or these buses, which carry tourists to the Palácio da Bolsa, to the Church of São Francisco and to Clérigos Tower? All these imposing buildings which stretch granitically upwards to the skies? This sett paving? Would he call us witches? Eccentrics?

I looked at my watch and I let out a scream that crashed against the watch face. I was late! Outside, the sky calmed its fury, making the pedestrian crossings visible.

Susana Fonseca

Final remark: A reference to John Whitehead (1726-1802). He was a man of many interests and talents: amateur architect, engineer, scientist (astronomer, mathematician and investigator), bibliophile (he owned a vast library) and British Consul. He lived in Porto between 1756 and 1802.

MONUMENTAL PORTO

01

02

03

01- "Meninos - A Abundância",

by Henrique Moreira

02- "Menina Nua - A Juventude",

by Henrique Moreira

03- "O Ardina", by Manuel Dias

04- "D. Pedro IV", by Célestin Anatole Calmels

05- Kiosk and Esplanade

06- Porto Town Hall

→ (from top to bottom)

01- Avenida dos Aliados

02- Detail of a granite building

04

05

To walk along **Avenida dos Aliados** is to feel the beat of the city with all its magnificence, throbbing from the beautiful façades, the wide pavements, the Town Hall building, the statues of different periods and, most of all, from the people who give life to the avenue, site of the celebrations of the city's main events. Located downtown, it is a place to go ideally on foot. The buildings are made of granite, but they present different characteristics which surprise us with the feeling that we are travelling in time. Today, some of these buildings belonging to banks share their space with cafés and esplanades, shops and kiosks.

The wide central portion of this avenue is paved with granite setts. In 2006, the avenue was completely reformulated along designs by the architects Álvaro Siza Vieira and Eduardo Souto de Moura.

06

← pages 34 / 35 Porto Town Hall

Tram outside Carmo Church

Tram at Rua de Santa Catarina

The **tram** is a pleasant way to travel round town and nowadays transports mainly tourists through the city. At the end of the 19th century, however, it provided the main link between Porto and its suburbs.

In 1872, the population came to know the speed of what were then called americanos (horse-drawn vehicles on tracks, which originated in America, hence their name, carrying people and goods). In 1895 the first electric trams appeared in the city.

There are currently 3 regular tourist routes:

Route 1 (Passeio Alegre / Infante), Route 18 (Massarelos / Carmo) and Route 22 (Carmo / Batalha). To those who enjoy watching the scenery of the city and the River Douro, this is the ideal form of transport, which might even include a visit to the Tram Museum.

→ *(from top to bottom)*

01- Tram at Miragaia

02- Tram parade

Tile panel - the History of Transports

Egas Moniz presenting himself to the King of León

São Bento Railway Station, located on Praça de Almeida Garrett, mirrors a part of the country's history, especially on the walls of the main atrium. The railway station was built in the beginning of the 20th century, on the site of the Convent of S. Bento de Ave-Maria. Its façade is magnificent and the atrium is covered with 20 000 tiles, a remarkable work by the painter Jorge Colaço. The panels represent several scenes, not only from Portuguese history but also from the history of transport. It is considered one of the world's most beautiful railway stations.

Façade of the Railway station and Praça de Almeida Garrett

→ (from top to bottom)

01- Station concourse

02- Main atrium

Hall of Nations

Portrait Room

Façade of the Palácio da Bolsa

Palácio da Bolsa is the headquarters and property of Porto Commercial Association, established in 1834. At that time, Queen D. Maria II authorised the construction of the Palace on the old ruins of São Francisco Convent. Hence, the oldest Business Association of Porto began its days in a site more suited to promoting the "Prosperity and Illustration" of the business community.

With a magnificent granite façade and neoclassical style architecture, the Palácio da Bolsa is one of the city's most attractive places.

Each room has different characteristics that embellish them and given then a historical context. The Arab Room and the Hall of Nations take us back to times of grandeur and prosperity.

Arab Room

Grand Staircase

General Meeting room

São Francisco Church

Portal of the Chapel of Nossa Senhora da Soledade

Catacombs Cemetery

Entering **São Francisco Church** is a fascinating experience of wonder given the decorations in giltwood carving and the exquisite beauty of the details of its three naves: the central, highest nave is illuminated by the light which enters through the rose window and reaches as far as the high altar.

São Francisco Church has been a National Monument since 1910, and it is the only church with Gothic architecture in town. It was integrated in the convent of the Observant Friars of Saint Francis, a convent that disappeared following a fire during the Siege of Porto. São Francisco Church was rebuilt and improved on various occasions between the 17th and 18th centuries, to the point where today it is considered one of the richest and most beautiful repositories of Baroque giltwood carvings. Especially noteworthy is the retable that represents "The Tree of Jesse" carved in polychrome wood.

→ (from top to bottom)

01- High Altar

02- "Tree of Jesse" retable

03- Carneiro Family Chapel

↑ ↗ *Interior of the Church*

Clérigos Tower is one of Porto's main icons. It was built between 1754 and 1763 under the supervision of Nicolau Nasoni, and includes the church which is also part of the eponymous monument. The tower is 75 metres high and presents on six floors, accessed through a staircase with 240 steps. It is decorated with Baroque motifs and sculptures of saints, and includes cornices and balustrades. The materials used on its construction were, essentially, granite and marble. Another curious fact about this monument is that the initial project foresaw the construction of two towers, not just one.

It is worth climbing up to the last floor to enjoy the magnificent view over the city and the River Douro.

View from the top of the Tower

→ *Clérigos Tower and Tram*

Since 1906 **Lello Bookshop** has been the haunt of men of letters and the arts, the inspiration for famous authors, the setting for literary gatherings but also a tranquil bookshop.

Classified as a monument of public interest, it was recognised internationally as one of the most beautiful bookshops in the world by "The Guardian", and as the coolest one by "Time". This bookshop is admired daily by thousands of visitors who throng to enter this magnificent example of Portuguese eclectic architecture, designed along plans by the engineer Xavier Esteves.

Outside, note the neo-gothic façade and two paintings by José Bielman. Inside, are unique decorative elements, such as the imposing staircase, the stained glass expanse of the skylight inscribed with the motto "Decus in Labore", Dignity in Labour, the ceilings with their gold stuccoed mouldings and the masonry work, all iconic elements of this bookshop.

Over the years this place has established its position as an important, authentic temple of art, science and culture.

MONUMENTAL PORTO

Churches of Carmelitas and Carmo

Congregados Church

Lapa Church

Soares dos Reis National Museum

Portuguese Centre of Photography

Almas Chapel

Praça do Infante D. Henrique and Statue of Infante D. Henrique

Ferreira Borges Market was built in 1885 and is an important example of cast-iron architecture. It currently houses the Hard Club, a multicultural venue for music, art, cinema and literature, as well as retail areas and a food court.

Ferreira Borges Market

Porto Customs House was built in the mid-19th century and is one of the city's largest infrastructures. At the end of the 20th century it underwent requalification and restoration works. Currently it hosts the Museum of Transports and Communications as well as a Congress Centre.

Porto Customs House

Ceuta café

"Piolho" café

Guarany café

Progresso café

The historical coffeehouses of Porto are emblematic places to visit today. Downtown, one can find a few which stand out for their cultural dimension, and they host diverse events, such as social gatherings, book launches, art exhibitions and recitals. One of the most famous cafes is Majestic on Rua de Santa Catarina, not only due to the fine service, but also because of the architectural beauty of the building. Good taste and style make this coffeehouse one of the most popular, particularly with tourists. Also packed with history and with a particular style of beauty is Guarany on Avenida dos Aliados.

Note also Café Ceuta in Rua de Ceuta, which dates from the 1950s, and Café Piolho in Praça Parada Leitão, famous for its thriving student community. Another example is Café Progresso, not far from Praça Carlos Alberto, which was recently remodelled but has managed to keep its identity, now with a more modern and cosmopolitan nature. One of the features of this place is that it still offers the delicious "filtered coffee". The coffeehouses with history have been a part of the city's cultural and bohemian life. Some of Porto's history was also made and written in these places.

Majestic café

Progresso café

Rua de Santa Catarina

Casa Oriental (grocery shop)

A Pérola do Bolhão (grocery shop)

Porto is a city that preserves its past, as one can verify by the number of traditional markets that are still open, particularly downtown. At **Bolhão Market** one can find the freshest produce, from vegetables to flowers, fish and meat. In the typical grocery shops such as *Pérola do Bolhão* or *Casa Chinesa*, the offer available includes nuts and dried fruits, codfish, cheese or coffee, among others. One's eye is immediately drawn to the architectural richness of these places. Here one can savour the magic and the joy of those who have known each other for a long time, as seller or customer. There is great camaraderie between those who work there and those who visit the market, whether to shop or merely to enjoy the embracing environment, with its characteristic colours and odours. Despite the existence of large shopping centres surrounding the city, traditional markets still play their community role.

Casa Chinesa (grocery shop)

Bolhão Market

Casa da Música

Look for me. I live in the most unlikely places, here, there and everywhere. Recently, I've been fixed up with a permanent address with a postcode. Write to me.

Do you know houses with gardens? My house isn't quite like that. Some people even think it is strange for they don't understand it was especially made for me.

Outside, on spring days, there's a bustle of youthful skaters. It is a place of passage, unfenced, built in my own image.

Inside, there is always joy, beauty and symphony. Visit me. I wander through the corridors waiting for you to come. I spend several beats in my favourite room, where there's more life. It's the heart of my house. Boom boom, boom boom. It booms and echoes in many areas. It's the Suggia Room, a resplendent homage to a woman who enchanted so many people with the strings of her cello. Find me. I'll be amongst the clap clap clapping of the people who come here.
Follow me. Inside my house you will also find a labyrinth. Corners you will discover by instinct. Visit the room where the sun is garbed in all its finery. Climb up my scores. Walk down the steps of my gamut. Delight me.

Observe my transparent walls. Can you see me? I'm in the darkest chords or in the glittering smiles. I live under the skin of the artists and on the trebles of the violins.

All you have here is the search. I will wait for you.

Now, shhhh. The concert is about to begin. Listen to me.

Susana Fonseca

VIP Room

Staircase

Façade of Casa da Música

Suggia Room

← pages 56 / 57- Casa da Música

Casa da Música was designed by the Dutch architect Rem Koolhaas as part of Porto 2001 – European Culture Capital. However, it was only inaugurated in 2005, and immediately became an icon of the city. The building has two auditoriums, as well as several areas for music-related activities. Sala Suggia is the main room of Casa da Música and its name pays homage to Guilhermina Medin Suggia (1885–1950), a famous Porto cellist. Another noteworthy space is the VIP Room, a small multifunctional area decorated with tiles reproducing original panels, which can be found in Portuguese and Dutch museums. At the top of the building there is also a third space intended for shows. We also recommend a visit to the restaurant, which has an amazing view over the city of Porto.

The architecture of the building was internationally acclaimed. Nicolai Ouroussoff, New York Times architecture critic, once said that from the building's original aspect alone one could see that this was one of the most important concert halls built in the last 100 years. The best way to know the building, which is shaped like a diamond, is to take a guided tour, during which you will be told about the functionality of each room.

Casa da Música Metro Station

Burgo Building and Sculpture by José de Guimarães

Modern art is also present in the city of Porto, ripping the skies with lines that are impressive in their originality, or disembowelling the earth with works that modify the landscape. The Vodafone Porto building on Avenida da Boavista, by José António Barbosa and Pedro Guimarães, has enriched the city with its bold architectural lines. The Burgo building and the metro station at Casa da Música are works of reference of the architecture idealised by Eduardo Souto de Moura, an architect awarded the 2011 Pritzker Prize (the Nobel of Architecture). Note, also, the imposing Dragão Stadium, designed by the architect Manuel Salgado.

Barreiros Pharmacy

Vodafone Building

Dragão Stadium

Liquidambar Avenue

Serralves Foundation, considered a cultural centre par excellence, consists of the Park, the Villa and the Contemporary Art Museum. It promotes concerts, guided tours, performances and workshops. However, Serralves is also the perfect place to have breakfast or even lunch. Afterwards, we recommend a visit to the gardens, where you can stroll and view a range of different species of trees and flowers, or simply sit on a park bench and catch up on your reading. Serralves Villa, an example of Art Deco architecture, was classified as a building of public interest. The small lakes opposite the Villa, together with the modernist-inspired environment, offer an atmosphere of beauty and freshness.

In Serralves one breathes culture, but one also feels nature and concern for the environment. For that reason, the Foundation organises several educational activities such as guided tours of the property and flora identification, and the annual event "Serralves em Festa" (Party at Serralves), during which the Foundation opens its doors to the community with a range of suggestions for both children and adults.

Trowel, Claes Oldenburg and Coosje Van Bruggen

Serralves Villa

Interior of Serralves Villa

Meadow

Rose Garden

Detail of the Rose Garden

Library

Interior access

Designed by the architect Siza Vieira (awarded the Pritzker Prize in 1992), **Serralves Museum** is already considered internationally as a reference in contemporary art exhibitions. Its main goals include the constitution of a collection representative of Portuguese and international contemporary art, the presentation of an agenda for temporary exhibitions, both collective and individual, and the organisation of educational programmes. The museum's permanent collection includes the works of several top artists from the late 60s. Also notable is the Library, which specialises in research in the areas of Contemporary Art, Architecture, Nature and Landscaping. Another asset is the Auditorium, which hosts a range of activities, such as cinema, dance, theatre and seminars.

Serralves museum

↑ ↓ City Park

Porto's City Park is one of Portugal's largest urban parks, with large grassed areas, wooded expanses and four lakes.

This park is geared to leisure activities, there is a fitness circuit, a picnic spot and a space for activities and traditional games. It is also an excellent place for watching a variety of bird species.

Another attraction is the Water Pavilion. It offers experiences aiming to demonstrate the importance of water for life, the many ways in which water is used and the different environments where water is present.

City Park (Water Pavilion)

Botanical Garden (Andresen House and rose garden)

Botanical Garden (Lakes' Garden)

Botanical garden

Inside Quinta do Campo Alegre, we recommend a visit to the **Botanical Garden**, whose beauty leaves no one indifferent. It presents very diverse spaces, dominated by the elegant shape of the Andresen House and also by the romantic garden.

Another green space worthy of attention is João Chagas Garden - better known as **Cordoaria Garden**. As well as a lake, there are several statues: "Flora" (1904), by António Teixeira Lopes; "Ramalho Ortigão" (1909), by Leopoldo de Almeida; "António Nobre" (1926), by Tomás da Costa; and "Thirteen Laughing at Each Other" (2001), by Juan Muñoz. This garden is located near Clérigos Tower, the Portuguese Centre of Photography, and Santo António Hospital.

→ *Cordoaria Garden*
"Thirteen Laughing at Each Other" by Juan Muñoz

Panoramic view of the gardens at Palácio de Cristal

Garden of Sentiments

Viewpoint

Solar do Vinho do Porto

The first building called **Porto Crystal Palace** was constructed for the purpose of hosting exhibitions. It was inaugurated in 1865 and later demolished in 1951 to make way for the present day Pavilhão Multiusos (Multiuse Pavilion), named Rosa Mota Pavilion.

The gardens surrounding the pavilion offer a privileged view over the River Douro and are well worth a visit. In addition to the many flowers and trees you will also find Almeida Garrett Library.

Close by the Palace, at Quinta da Macieirinha, you will find the Romantic Museum, a reconstitution of the interior of a middle-class 19th century house; and Tait House, which presents temporary exhibitions in an impressive setting where green combines with the blue of the sky and we see glimpses of the River Douro.

Almeida Garrett Library

Garden

Dragão Stadium

Celebrating a Porto F. C. victory

D'Bandada

Primavera Sound

Throughout each year the city organises several events which fill the streets with new colours, joy and movement. At the start of the summer people traditionally take part in the Primavera Sound Festival and as summer ends the Baixa resonates with the music of the D'Bandada festival. The Boavista Circuit is a biannual event that takes place in summer on Avenida da Boavista, where fans of motor car races can watch their favourite drivers doing their utmost to win. Several spontaneous celebrations occur in Avenida dos Aliados, including those of Futebol Clube do Porto, which celebrates its victories downtown every time it wins a championship or a trophy. On that occasion, white and blue are the predominant colours.

Red Bull Air Race

Boavista Circuit (historic grand prix)

Men grilling sardines at Fontaínhas

Cascade of São João (Ilha do Galo Preto)

Basil and garlic flowers

Popular Dance near Porto Cathedral

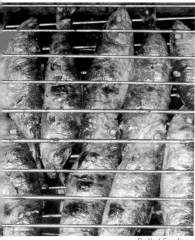

Grilled Sardines

Cascade of São João (Fontaínhas)

São João Hammer

"Ilha do Galo Preto"

Hammers of São João at Porto's Ribeira

São João air balloon

Fireworks at D. Luís I Bridge

Traditional parades - São João

São João do Porto is a unique celebration, in which the smell of grilled sardines permeates the typical streets and, as if by magic, the sky fills with small air balloons. The revellers, armed with leeks and plastic hammers, walk joyfully for miles.

In several neighbourhoods, such as Fontaínhas, Massarelos or Miragaia, there are small festivals with folk singers and enthusiastic dancers.

Fireworks at Douro River

The cascades and ornaments allusive to São João are a source of pride for the neighbourhood residents who that night eat dinner outside and offer sardines to passersby.

It's a Catholic celebration, with a strong profane component, which is celebrated on the night of 23rd to 24th June and marks the birth of St. John the Baptist. It is certainly the longest night in the city, where the rule is to walk through neighbourhoods and partake in improvised dances – from Passeio Alegre to Fontaínhas, passing through Ribeira, where at midnight one can watch the fireworks. Thousands of people travel to the Invicta to watch and participate in the city's main celebration. For many, the night ends at the beach as the sun is rising.

The celebrations end with the "Rusgas de São João", traditional parades that have recently been recovered. The representatives of the several parishes parade from Praça da Batalha to Avenida dos Aliados. There's always music and the scent of lemon balm, leeks and "manjerico" basil. There are baskets with grilled sardines, corn bread, smoked ham and wine to wash it all down. The revellers are dressed for the occasion, depicting the Porto of the past, and their jollity is contagious to those watching the singing and dancing in the moonlight.

Port Wine cellars

Port Wine, from left to the right: Tawny, Ruby and White

Casks for ageing Port Wine

On the **Vila Nova de Gaia** side of the river we find the cellars where the famous Port Wine from the Douro terraces is aged. Visiting these lodges is an unforgettable experience. We also suggest a walk by the River Douro along the so called Cais de Gaia, which has a dazzling view of Porto's Ribeira. However, there is much more to see and enjoy in Gaia. For instance, the Biological Park and Santo Inácio Zoo deserve a visit due to the diversity of animals one can find there. To those who enjoy outdoor sports, Lavandeira Park is a good option, and to those who prefer the sea, Gaia offers a coastline that is over 15 km long. If you decide to visit the city's historical centre, it is worth going up to Serra do Pilar – a World Heritage Site – which one can now reach on the cable car that connects it with the riverside area.

Beach and Chapel of Senhor da Pedra

Porto's metro and Serra do Pilar

Cais de Gaia (Quay of Gaia)

Matosinhos Beach

Matosinhos Town Centre

With a strong link to the sea and to fishing activities, **Matosinhos** is a city full of history and cultural heritage. This municipality has several places that are worth visiting, such as Quinta de Santiago, the Monastery of Leça do Balio and the Fort of Nossa Senhora das Neves. In 2007 Matosinhos acquired a new iconic landmark which embellishes one of the entrances of the city: a giant sea anemone - a sculpture by the American artist Janet Echelman - made from fishing net. The municipality is also known for its celebrations in honour of Senhor de Matosinhos, which attract thousands of visitors.

In gastronomic terms, there are several restaurants where lovers of good fish can indulge themselves.

→ *(from top to bottom)*

01- Leixões Terminal cruise

02- "She Changes", by Janet Echelman

Sea Salt

I seek silence and freedom in the days that succeed each other, almost unchangingly, except for the sun, the rain or the wind. I am indifferent to the severity of its gusts.

There are days when everything surrounds me. The past is made of ghosts who settle on these waters and talk to me of the old days. We speak of the joy of coming to harvest the salt. We share stories about the families.

A son who was born; a woman who recovered from a serious illness; an uncle who came back rich from Brazil; a kid who came top in his school's exam and even a cat we managed to rescue from the roof without damaging the animal or the tiles. Stories from a past that no longer belongs to me.

My reality is the salt that I harvest from the salt pans - the salt flower, formed by the crystals which form on the surface of the water. If I don't harvest it in time and with care, it will sink to the bottom and become ordinary sea salt.

Yesterday, when I got home, my youngest goddaughter was waiting for me at the door. She had arrived from Porto to do a school project, and wanted me to take her to the city centre on Sunday. After endless pleading, with a tear in her eye, she finally gave up, but I cleaned her face and asked her not to waste the salt of her tears for so little.

When the day arrived, I took her to the centre. We took a ride on a BUGA and walked along the canals. I showed her the moliceiros and its paintings. We went to a pastry shop and I bought her a Pipinha de Ovos-Moles, with striped houses painted on it. She laughed, saying that they looked like pyjama houses. I explained that those houses were located in Costa Nova and promised her that, one day, I would take her there; but, at that moment, I wanted to show her something of my life.

Once back at the salt pans, where the tides imbibe the water from the Ria, we remained between the silence and the world.

I showed her the small mountains of white gold, essential to our life. In that place, everything was just as it should be. I explained to her that nowhere else could the sun be seen from one horizon to the other. The salt was harvested from those rectangles with know-how and love. She felt the wind on her face and understood the freedom reflected on the waters. White tears came to her eyes.

Susana Fonseca

Cais do Botirão

Cultural and Congress Centre of Aveiro

Naïf painting of a Moliceiro Boat

→ *Casa Major Pessoa - Art Nouveau Museum of Aveiro, the most representative building of this style in the city*

There are many cities that enjoy the privilege of being near water. **Aveiro** is no exception, as it stands out thanks to its famous Ria (estuary) with its abundance of fish and water birds.

The moliceiros, unique boats with a simple decoration reminiscent of naïf paintings, are also connected to the Ria, and they continue to gather sea grasses, or "moliço" – excellent fertilizer for barren lands. In addition to the Ria and its surroundings, Aveiro district also has beautiful beaches, namely S. Jacinto. The architecture is a representative element of the city as well, with particular emphasis on the Art Nouveau façades.

For those who enjoy outdoor activities, take a tour on the moliceiro, ride a BUGA (free-use bicycles in Aveiro) or try one of the several nautical sports. Gastronomically speaking, Aveiro is known for its fish dishes and, in confectionery, for the famous ovos moles, a delicacy made from sweet egg yolk paste.

← *pages 80 / 81- "Palheiros", Costa Nova Houses*

Marinha da Troncalhada Ecomuseum

A note about the University of Aveiro, which was founded in 1973 and rapidly became one of the most dynamic and innovative Portuguese universities. Its campus constitutes a 'mini-town' surrounded by the natural beauty of the salt pans, with a view of the Ria, not far from the city centre. The institution is annually visited by hundreds of tourists who enjoy its singular architecture with buildings designed by the award-winning architects Álvaro Siza Vieira and Eduardo Souto de Moura.

The guided tours to the Santiago da Fonte Salt Pan, owned by the University of Aveiro, allow visitors to discover this outdoor cultural landscape and the different types of artisanal salt produced and extracted from it. Furthermore, there is a restored dual-purpose warehouse: providing support for the salt production and developing scientific and didactic activities, but also promoting accessible tourism.

"Palheiros", Costa Nova houses

Barra Lighthouse

Dunes at Barra Beach

Known for the Vista Alegre porcelain industry, the city of **Ílhavo** is also identified by the Farol da Barra - the tallest of Portugal's 48 Portuguese maritime lighthouses, located in Barra, in the parish of Gafanha da Nazaré. Also famous is the extensive shore of the Costa Nova do Prado beach. Another attraction is the typical houses of this beach - the Palheiros. They are characterised by their wooden façades, painted in bright joyful striped colours, alternating with white. As far as gastronomy is concerned, we recommend the bread of Vale de Ílhavo, made in an artisanal way and baked in a wood-burning oven.

Castle of Santa Maria da Feira

The "Imaginarius" festival

↑ ↗ ↙ Medieval Journey in the Land of Santa Maria

Santa Maria da Feira is a municipality with strong cultural traditions and it has focused on promoting the events that take place during the year. The Medieval Fair – one of the most important nationwide -; Imaginarius – an event of unique quality in the performing arts and one of the main references of Portugal's street theatre -; and the Festa das Fogaceiras, a secular tradition and the municipality's most emblematic festivity, are good examples. As regards the cultural buildings, the highlight goes to the truly amazing medieval castle and to the congress centre, *Europarque*, which also plays host to an extensive and qualified cultural agenda.

Espinho Beach

Fishing boat

Espinho's Multimeios Centre

Fishing boat

The city of **Espinho** has attracted a wide range of visitors, whether for its points of interest, for its gastronomy and casino, or for the animated cinema festival, CINANIMA, which has an excellent reputation. The region's cultural offering is diverse: worth a visit, for example, are the Multimeios Centre or the Municipal Museum, focusing on the fishing community and the canning industry of Espinho. This museum seeks to characterise the Bairro da Marinha and the Arte da Xávega and to demonstrate the place of the Brandão Gomes Canning Plant in the context of national and international canning. Its beaches are also famous and for many years have been attracting hundreds of tourists who, during the season, stroll along the streets of this small town.

Harbour of Póvoa de Varzim

Tile panels representing fishing activities

A city that is contemporary in its makeup but also had older quarters, **Póvoa do Varzim** enjoys a rich and diverse fish cuisine. Located on a sandy coastal plain, the city benefits from a temperate maritime microclimate, which is why it is very popular in the summer both with the region's inhabitants and with tourists, especially due to its pleasant beaches. Its connection to the sea is also represented in tile panels - true works of art that portray fishermen's everyday life. In addition, this northern city is also known for its bull ring. The *Junqueira* area is pleasant for a walk and, at Avenida dos Banhos, you may find discos, bars and esplanades. Póvoa Casino, located in a neoclassical style building, is another attraction of the city.

Riverside area, 16th Century Carrack and Convent of Santa Clara

Fort of São João Baptista

Vila do Conde Aqueduct

Vila do Conde, a city known for its fishing harbour and beautiful beaches, is also rich in architectural and cultural heritage. At its very entrance, we are surprised by the Aqueduct - an artificial canal, which initially had 999 arches, built from its source to the Convent of Santa Clara. Although no longer continuous, a great part of the original structure still remains. Among the several monuments which deserve a visit, we highlight the 16th Carrack, as well as the Fort of S. João. Fishing and fish-related activities still prevail in Caxinas.

Vila do Conde is also known for the famous bobbin lace and its lace-makers. Due to its privileged geographic location, this city offers its visitors a variety of delicious fish and shellfish dishes.

Lovers' Handkerchiefs

It was a slow afternoon, like those that warn us that time is something we must respect. Time does not always pass as we would like it to and I had to study for a university exam, but I was somehow more inclined to distraction. My mother knocked on the door, arousing me from a state in which I was almost drowning in a flood of thoughts that always brought back his image to me, in an uncontrollable whirlpool. Softly she asked me if she could interrupt, as my head was buried in a book. She had a box in her hand to show me. I had already seen several 'lovers' handkerchiefs' for sale in handicraft shops, but I had never paid them much attention. My hands took that small square of timeless embroidered cloth that lay in its box.

My mother explained that that handkerchief had been embroidered by her grandmother: "Back then relationships were not like today. Your great-grandmother used to sew by the window. One day, she noticed that a small pebble had been lightly thrown against the window. She took a peep and glimpsed a young man who fascinated her with his charming smile. From then on, the young man would come by in the evenings. Sometimes he threw her a flower, a shell or a coloured pebble; other times he just walked slowly and whistled. Until one day she surprised him by throwing him this handkerchief, which he started to wear round his neck. At that moment, their hearts overflowed with joy, for they both knew they would be married."

As my mother left the room, I stared at that handkerchief, tenderly embroidered with hearts, keys and a dove with a letter in its beak. Almost without noticing it, I copied the quatrain embroidered on the handkerchief into my notebook, although not the misspellings: "Here is my heart/ and the key to open its door / I have nothing more to give you/ And you have nothing more to ask me for."

The simplicity and the purity of those gestures and that love showed me what I had not wanted to see. I forgot the slowness of time, deleted his mobile phone number and smiled once more.

Susana Fonseca

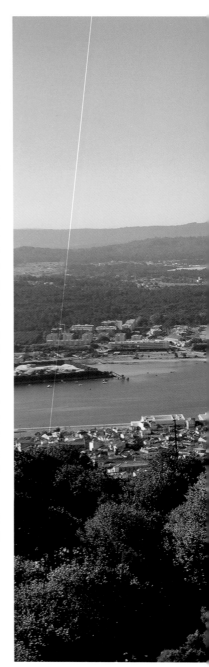

Interior of Santa Luzia Temple

Viana do Castelo is a city of unparalleled beauty and one of its landmarks is undoubtedly the Sanctuary or Temple of the Sacred Heart of Jesus, better known as Temple of Santa Luzia. The interior of this monument was inspired by Sacré-Coeur Basilica, in Montmartre, Paris. This amazing temple is located at the top of the Santa Luzia hill, where one is presented with an astonishing view over the region, which combines sea, river (the Lima) and a large mountain range. A place where our gaze is touched by such beauty.

In the centre of the city, we find the Praça da República Fountain. It is a Renaissance work by the Porto stonemason, João Lopes, located at the eastern side of the square - in front of the old Town Hall. Included in Viana do Castelo's extensive natural, cultural and architectural heritage, we have also to mention the Eiffel Bridge, by Gustave Eiffel. Inaugurated on 30 June 1878, it is an example of cast-iron architecture.

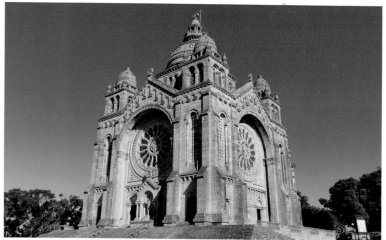

Santa Luzia Temple

← pages 90 / 91

Viana do Castelo

Viana Cathedral

Railway station

Praça da República fountain

Viana do Castelo Eiffel bridge

Procession to the River and the Sea

In **Viana do Castelo** municipality there are annually about 70 feasts and pilgrimages, of which we highlight the Festivities of Nossa Senhora d'Agonia, in August, which attract thousands of tourists from all over the world. From 20 August until the weekend, Viana is filled with colours and joy and, in the streets one sees bagpipe players, *Zés-pereiras* [large drum players], gigantones and cabeçudos (giants and big heads). On the morning of the 20th, the procession to the sea takes place. However, it is the Parade of the Mordomas (or young girls) that officially opens the festivities, with hundreds of local women dressed in their traditional costumes with lots of gold jewellery round their neck and on their chest. The high point of the festivities is the Historical and Ethnographic Parade, during which one can see the allegorical floats. The last day is the day of the Costume Party, where women wear their embroidered outfits, representing life in the country and in town. Enhancing the beauty of the parade are women donning black velvet and satin dresses. The scarves covering their heads are made of pure silk and the socks of white cotton. The gold and the sparkling glass beads are part of the costume. The nights are lit up by the fireworks, cascading from the bridge and lighting up the city sky.

Pilgrimage of Nossa Senhora d'Agonia (zés-pereiras)

Traditional Costume

Image of Nossa Senhora d'Agonia

Traditional Costume

Fishing boat at River Minho

Fountain in Largo do Terreiro

Parish Church

In the far north of Portugal you will find the municipality of **Caminha**, about 25 km from Viana do Castelo. Visitors are presented with a mosaic of vegetation, magnificent beaches, hills and rivers - Minho, Coura and Âncora. In Caminha, we recommend a visit to the Parish Church, as well as to the Clock Tower where one can get to know the historical centre better.

One of the striking places is the Ínsua, a rocky islet which divides the mouth of the River Minho. There, one can find the ruins of a convent, a church and a lighthouse, within a fortress.

There are several handicraft sellers in this region, giving it an authentic ambience.

Some of the region's typical dishes are Caldeirada de Peixe (fish stew), Arroz de Lampreia (lamprey rice) and Solha Seca de Lanhelas (smoked dried plaice). There is also a wide range of confectionery on offer.

You can enjoy a walk along the walking trails or a kayak ride and practice water ski or scuba diving.

Vila Nova de Cerveira, River Minho and Ilha dos Amores (Lovers' Island)

River Minho

"O Cervo" (stag) at Alto do Crasto

Historical centre

Located in Upper Minho, **Vila Nova de Cerveira** used to be a land of deer, fallow deer and does. Today it is a nice town, surrounded by magnificent landscapes, from which one can see the sculpture of a large deer on the hilltop, by Mestre José Rodrigues.

Vila Nova de Cerveira is part of a region where protected areas can be found, such as the National Ecological Reserve, which makes it a privileged place for the discovery of walking trails.

This town is also known as the Arts Town because of the biennial festival which has been taking place there since 1986. In the town, note the 14th century historical centre.

Brejoeira Palace

Brejoeira Palace (gardens)

Centre of Monção, Praça Deuladeu Martins

The municipality of **Monção** nestles in the extensive and fertile valley of the River Minho and the mountainous escarpments. In addition to the village's historical centre, you should also visit Lapela Tower, what remains of a medieval castle and its walls.

The sumptuous *Brejoeira* Palace, in neoclassical style, located about 6 km from Monção, is a supreme example of noble residences in Portugal. Its interior contains majestic rooms with distinctive decoration. The grounds of the palace produce the famous *Alvarinho* wine.

As far as celebrations are concerned, from time immemorial a combat has taken place on Corpus Christi day, between St. George and the Coca, an imaginary monster. This fight is staged in *Praça de Deuladeu* and symbolises the victory of Good over Evil.

Of the several gastronomic specialities, we highlight the convent delicacies, such as *"barriguinhas de freira"*. Another delicacy, this time for the eyes, is the contact with the wonderful landscapes, which you can discover along the various walking trails.

↑↓ *Valença Fort*

Valença Fort

Due to its proximity with Spain, **Valença** acts as a place for tourist shopping and conviviality between the two countries. Two of the city's attractions are the landscape next to River Minho and the hundred year old iron bridge, an Eiffel model, a jewel of European industrial archaeology. Its historical centre, located in the interior of a former stronghold, is surrounded by walls which extend over five kilometres. For those who enjoy outdoor sports, Valença has a greenway, which has attracted visitors of many nationalities. Along this corridor, which follows the course of the River Minho, you can go jogging, skating or cycling, to name just a few.

Keep of the Castle of Melgaço

General view of Melgaço

Centre of Melgaço

Melgaço is a castled town located near the River Minho and not far from Spain. The main attractions worth a visit are the Keep, surrounded by a circular wall, and the Parish Church, in Romanesque style. The ancient origins of Melgaço can be verified in places like Parada do Monte, Gave or in the plateau of Castro Laboreiro, where one finds megalithic graves and burial mounds. There are also several convents, chapels and churches, of which we highlight the Church of Nossa Senhora da Orada.

Melgaço is also known for the practice of adventure sports and ecotourism-oriented activities: rafting, rappel, zip wire, canoeing and archery. You can also choose to go for a walk, a horse ride, or a bicycle ride. The typical dishes are directly connected with the region's characteristic ingredients. We highlight the Cabrito Assado (roast kid), Lampreia com arroz à bordalesa (lamprey with bordelaise rice), trutas do rio Minho abafadas (River Minho marinated trout) and sarrabulho (a dish with meat and pig's blood).

River Vez

Parish Church

Town Hall

Surrounded by verdant nature and bathed by River Vez, **Arcos de Valdevez** is located within the Peneda-Gerês National Park. It is a small charming village thanks to its typical streets and several characteristic houses and manor-houses, from which stands out the *Casa do Terreiro*, currently known by *Casa das Artes*.

A walk through the historical centre should include a visit to the several churches, such as the Church of Nossa Senhora da Lapa, in a Baroque style, and the Main Church; the bridge over River Vez; and the Monument in Honour of the Skirmish of Valdevez, from the authorship of José Rodrigues. If you choose to go to the former *Campo da Feira*, next to the river, you may admire a magnificent landscape made of hills and valleys.

The region's gastronomy is typically from Minho, and it includes the *Cozido à Minhota* [boiled pork with vegetables and sausages] and the *Rojões* [pork morsels], always followed by the green wines. On the confectionery, we highlight the *Charutos de Ovos* [sweet egg rolls] and the *Cavacas dos Arcos* [eggs and sugar delicacy].

Bridge over the River Lima

↑ ↗ *Pillory and Old Market*

Ponte da Barca, located in a region where nature reigns supreme, owes its name to the barge that used to make the crossing between the two banks of the River Lima and later also to the bridge (ponte), which made the journeys easier. Its architectural heritage includes the Castle and the Parish Church. We also recommend a visit to the *Lindoso Espigueiros* or hórreos (granaries) and to the church of the former Monastery of *Bravães*, in Romanesque style. This municipality is known for its festivities and pilgrimages, an important one being the Pilgrimage of St. Bartholomew that takes place in August. A range of activities is organised throughout the six days, which include traditional games and challenge singing competitions. Gastronomically speaking, this region is known for its Papas de Sarrabulho and Serra Amarela kid. As far as confectionery is concerned, great favourites are the White Cake, Rabanadas de Mel (fried bread slices with honey) and *"Magalhães"* (made with honey and nuts), in honour of the explorer Ferdinand Magellan who performed the first circumnavigation of the earth. It is believed that he was born here in this town filled with history.

Bridge over the River Lima

Local tradition of Vaca das Cordas

Praça de Camões

Ponte de Lima, Portugal's oldest town, is located by the River Lima, from which it acquired its name.
The best-known postcard of the town is one showing the bridge over the river, a true work of art combining the medieval and Roman styles. Directly opposite the bridge is the historical centre, with its Torre da Cadeia (Prison Tower), attesting to the fact that this town was once a small walled citadel. Currently, *Torre da Cadeia* houses the Tourist Office. Ponte de Lima is also known for its market days and feasts, such as the Horse Fair, held in June or July, and the International Garden Festival, which takes place every year from May to October. The so-called *Feiras Novas* (or new fairs) are the municipality's most famous celebrations, which include concertina toccatas, musical bands, livestock competitions and parades.

Vaca das Cordas is a famous tradition in the region, which takes place in June, in the late afternoon. The cow (nowadays a wild bull), starts the race outside the gate of *Nossa Senhora de Aurora* House, in the historical centre. The animal is then steered to the Parish Church, and should run round it three times, to respect tradition.

The Roses of Guimarães

I walked tthrough the city centre as in times past Dona Isabel had breached the wall around the castle. Proud and confident, I carried a bunch of roses to offer my beloved to stop him going off to war. As with life the roses were fragile, but thorny as well.

I sat at an esplanade in Praça da Oliveira. I was in front of the Padrão do Salado. I felt the weight of history and hoped to succeed in my quest. I asked for a sparkling water, as I waited for him to arrive and grant me a few moments of his attention. He sat opposite me and asked why I had brought roses. I remembered I had picked them to give him when I made my request. As I left my garden with no one to turn to I wanted to stop him going to the other end of the world. However, once again, he was quite firm about his decision; he would leave with his company at the end of the following week. Our relationship had been put on the backburner.
I left him half the bunch of roses and got up. Our life had been beautiful, but it ended because of the thorns.

I felt defeated. Unlike Dona Isabel, I couldn't try to convince the opponent not to fight this battle. With tears in my eyes, I walked through the square and down Rua Santa Maria. I thought of stopping at Praça de Santiago, but it was too close. The narrow streets, with clothes hanging at the windows, squeezed my heart. My hands tore the petals and dropped then as I walked, leaving a trail of sorrow in my wake.

Before I knew it, I was in Largo do Toural and on my way to the Palace of the Dukes of Bragança. I stopped in front of the sign: "Here Portugal was born". Suddenly, I turned around and saw him. He was looking at me and smiling. I ran to him. "Here hope was reborn".

Odete Silva

Note: Reference to Dona Isabel de Lira, who, according to legend, stopped a battle between D. Fernando (Portugal) and D. Henrique de Trastâmara (Castile), in the 14th century.

Detail in Largo do Toural

Church of Nossa Senhora da Consolação e Santos Passos

"Here Portugal Was Born"

As "The Cradle City", **Guimarães** occupies a prominent place in the history of Portugal as a nation. In fact, according to tradition, it is believed that the first King of Portugal, D. Afonso Henriques, was born and baptised here. The historical centre, today classified as a World Heritage Site, sends us back to the time of the foundation of Portuguese nationhood, as recalled by the sign: "Here Portugal was born", on one of the towers along the wall. Inside the walls are the Castle and the Chapel of São Miguel, where D. Afonso Henriques was probably baptised. You can also visit the Church of Nossa Senhora da Oliveira, rebuilt in honour of the Virgin Mary after the victory at the Battle of Aljubarrota, and the Padrão do Salado, raised to give thanks for the victory in the battle of the same name.

Within that same area, note the Palace of the Dukes of Bragança, which dates from the 15th century and has been partially converted into a museum. Included in its many exhibits on display visitors may admire art works, tapestry and furniture of the 17th and 18th centuries.

← page. 104 / 105, D. Afonso Henriques

Guimarães Castle

Palace of the Dukes of Bragança

107

↑ ↓ ↘ Vila Flor Cultural Centre

Despite the marked presence of history, Guimarães has known how to combine past and present. To do so, it invested in modern, welcoming spaces, such as the City Park and the **Vila Flor Cultural Centre**. The latter resulted from the restoration of the old palace of the same name and hosts cultural events.

We also recommend a cable car ride to Penha Sanctuary, from where you can gaze down on Guimarães, chosen as 2012 European Culture Capital. Don't leave the Cradle City without tasting the typical Roast Kid and Guimarães pies.

Praça de Santiago

Largo da Oliveira

Rua de Santa Maria

Azulejo

Garden of Santa Bárbara

Arco da Porta Nova

Praça da República

The city of **Braga**, named *Bracara Augusta* by the Romans, has more than 2000 years of history. In the year 1070, D. Pedro, the first Bishop of Braga, organised the Diocese, driving the city's development. The city grew around the Cathedral. In a climate of great religious fervour over the centuries, monasteries, convents and churches were built. The city still maintains its prestige as the religious capital of the country. This is shown by the fact that the streets fill with people holding candles as they watch the impressive processions during Holy Week.

Arco da Porta Nova is the gateway into the city, which is also known for its splendid 18th century houses, its gardens and its parks. The garden of Santa Bárbara, for example, is located next to the medieval wing of Braga's Episcopal Palace. Biscaínhos Palace, which houses the Ethnography and Arts Museum, also has one of the most beautiful Baroque gardens in Portugal. There is extensive archaeological heritage, with particular emphasis on the Roman Baths in the parish of Cividade.

The **Cathedral**, located in one of the oldest Christian cities in the world, is considered a centre of episcopal diffusion. It is an important temple of the Portuguese Romanesque, although crossed with other architectural styles. It contains the Sacred Art Museum or Tesouro-Museu da Sé de Braga, a collection that is priceless, with items that range over a period of 1500 years, a synthesis of Christian life.

In addition to the Cathedral, we recommend a visit to the Monastery of Tibães. Its foundation predates the foundation of Portugal. In the 16th century, it became the motherhouse of the Benedictine congregation of Portugal and Brazil. Following a period of neglect it has been restored and hosts cultural events.

The religious architecture of Pópulo Church, the Chapel of the Coimbra family and of the Chapel of S. Frutuoso is worthy of appreciation.

Coffeehouse "A Brasileira" in the historical centre

Majestic processions during the Holy Week (farricocos / fogaréus)

Sanctuary of Sameiro

Stairway and Sanctuary of Bom Jesus do Monte

Basilica of Bom Jesus

The Sanctuary of Bom Jesus do Monte, or Sanctuary of **Bom Jesus de Braga**, is a religious and tourist place located in Tenões, a parish in Braga. The lush woods surrounding this Sanctuary provide both beauty and mysticism. The stairways, flanked by centuries-old trees, lead pedestrians from one chapel to the next, representing passages from the Passion of Christ. Halfway up, there is a viewpoint from which one can look down on the city. The space then widens and at the top one can see the Basilica of Bom Jesus. The Sanctuary of Sameiro is a Marian temple, in front of which there are stairs, topped by images of the Virgin Mary and the Sacred Heart of Jesus.

Barcelos Cockerels

Church of Bom Jesus da Cruz

Barcelos Medieval Bridge

Palace of the Counts of Barcelos

Barcelos, a city with millenary roots, is rich in heritage, legends and traditions. The most famous legend is associated with the cockerel which served to prove the innocence of a man, who had been unjustly accused. The Cross of Senhor do Galo, opposite the Parish Church, is also linked with the same legend. Over time, the cockerels became one of Portugal's symbols and they can be found in handicraft shops and in the weekly Fair of Barcelos. In the city's historical centre there are several monuments, which include the Palace of the Counts of Barcelos, where the Archaeology Museum is installed.

→ *Peneda Gerês National Park (Mata da Albergaria)*

Garrano horses

Barrosã cattle

Vilarinho das Furnas Dam

Church of São Bento da Porta Aberta

Roman milestones on the Roman road or Geira

Oak grove at Mata da Albergaria

Peneda Gerês National Park has several features and an abundant natural landscape to be explored. One such example can be found in the parish of Castro Laboreiro, located on the plateau of the same name, at the centre of the mountain range, within an extensive area of the National Park. Another example is the Garrano horse, a breed originating in Northern Portugal, and for centuries used as a pack horse and a working animal. Because of its size it is considered a pony. It currently lives in the semi-wild, in the areas of the Gerês and Cabreira mountains. Another point of interest is the Sanctuary of São Bento da Porta Aberta, which may have its origin in a hermitage built there around 1640. It used to provide shelter to passersby and its doors were always open, hence its name. The construction of the current Sanctuary began in 1880. Throughout Gerês, several milestones can still be seen along the Geira route - used by the Romans, which connected Astorga to Brácara.

The first National Park was created about forty years ago. With an area of over 72 thousand hectares Peneda Gerês National Park encompasses the municipalities of Melgaço, Arcos de Valdevez, Ponte da Barca, Terras do Bouro and Montalegre, and the mountain ranges of Peneda, Soajo, Amarela, Gerês, as well as the plateaus of Laboreiro and Mourela. Although dominated by oak trees, the forest is fairly diversified, and includes species such as holly, Portuguese laurel (*Prunus lusitanica*), birch, pine and arbutus. This park has many attractions, but the most popular are definitely the natural lagoons and Mata da Albergaria. The Gerês baths are also famous in Portugal for the therapeutic qualities of their waters.

My Douro

There were times when I thought the Douro was just a bunch of mountains where Port Wine was made!

However, when I first stepped into that boat at Cais de Gaia and slid through the Douro waters, I entered a different world. A world full of enigmatic mysteries, where silence roars louder than any city in full swing. I fell silent and looked around. I saw colours and landscapes impossible to describe on one single page. I had my camera, which goes with me everywhere, and I thought maybe with it I would be able to grasp the true Douro.

I travelled every hill in this region, I saw the magic of each village surrounded by vineyards, I saw men and women harvesting on the steep slopes, eagles conquering the skies, the grape treading feast, boats passing by filled with tourists, the train following the winding course of the river... Under snow and sun, with storms succeeded by calm, I saw the grapes budding, growing, being harvested, trodden and made into wine. I also went to the lodges where the wine waits for the optimum drinking moment and I tasted the nectar.

I saw the Douro... but whenever I try to recall those times in the valleys I call "my Douro", the photographs I took are never enough. The colours of those valleys don't fit in any spectrum, the joy of those people must be felt and experienced to be understood. There's something magical about that valley, something that can't be told, only felt.

Sérgio Fonseca

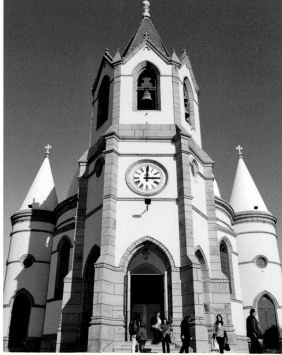

Sanctuary of Nossa Senhora da Piedade (Church of Sameiro)

Sameiro Garden

Penafiel Municipal Museum

Quinta da Aveleda

Monastery of Paço de Sousa

Penafiel is a municipality located in an environment made up by hills, valleys and rivers, where one can visit the Dolmen of Santa Marta, the Menhir of Luzim, rock engravings and necropoles. It is here in this region, in fact, that one can study one of the largest fortified settlements of the North-west of the Iberian Peninsula (Oldrões/Galegos) - a proto-Roman city. A reference, also, to the monuments included in the Romanesque Route of Vale do Sousa and Quinta da Aveleda, where you can taste its famous wines. Check out the historic centre of Penafiel and the Sanctuary of Nossa Senhora da Piedade (Sameiro). Also worth a visit is the Municipal Museum which in 2010 was considered Portugal's best museum.

The Fair of S. Martinho, which takes place every year from 10 to 20 November, is a unique fair, especially given its tradition of wine and chestnuts.

← pages 118 / 119, Quinta do Vesúvio

Church and Bridge of São Gonçalo over River Tâmega

What most characterises the city of **Amarante** is, without a doubt, its historical centre, where one can appreciate, among other buildings, *São Gonçalo* Bridge and the Monastery of *São Gonçalo*. If we fall into the embrace of this landscape, we will feel that it welcomes us with a blend of romanticism and spirituality.

Across the bridge and into the church, we perceive the devotion to Saint Gonçalo. One of the images of the saint can be found in the sacristy. Popular wisdom notes that anyone wishing to get married must pull the rope found on the image and make the wish.

We recommend a visit to the museum of the painter Amadeo de Souza-Cardoso, located near the monastery. Next, we suggest a walk by the banks of the River Tâmega or through the city's picturesque streets, where you will be able to see what is left of Magalhães Manor House, an 18th century building, as well as find confectionaries with dainty traditional delicacies.

Another point of interest in this municipality is *Casa de Pascoaes*, located in the parish of Gatão, home to the Portuguese poet Teixeira de Pascoaes.

Magalhães Manor House

São Gonçalo

Main façade reflected in the lake

Library

"Sala Rica"

The **Manor House of Mateus** is one of the most significant works of Portuguese architecture of the Baroque period. Built in the first half of the 17th century, it is formed by two buildings that are connected by two perpendicular corridors. This architectural whole is further embellished by the chapel, the New Winery (converted into a room for temporary exhibitions), the "Barrão da Eira" (the old barn), the statue by João Cutileiro (in the lake) and, above all, by the magnificent boxwood gardens in the French style. Visitors may choose between two types of visits: the general tour, which includes the house (with its priceless, distinctive contents) and the chapel, or simply a tour of the gardens. As well as exhibitions, Casa de Mateus promotes many cultural initiatives, namely music courses, concerts, conferences and seminars and also awards the D. Dinis Literary Prize.

Town Hall

Diogo Cão house

Largo do Pelourinho

Vila Real emerges on the plateau located at the junction of the Rivers Corgo and Cabril, surrounded by a beautiful natural landscape, dominated by the Alvão and Marão mountain ranges. One can safely say that it is the ideal starting point to explore the Douro Valley and follow the Port Wine Route. In the last few years, several cultural buildings were established in the city, such as the Vila Real Theatre, which have given it a new dynamic. Several zones were also restored, including the old quarter known as Bairro dos Ferreiros and the area around the River Corgo. Gastronomy is another strong feature of this region. We highlight the Tripas aos Molhos (veal tripe), Covilhetes (salted ham and beef pies) and the many spicy sausages. As for pastry, we highlight *Pastéis de Toucinho*, lard pies, Cristas de Galo (sweet pies with almonds and eggs), the convent pastries of *Santa Clara* and *Pitos de Santa Luzia* (pumpkin pies), to name just a few. It won't be difficult for you to find some of these delicacies on the city's picturesque streets.

Sanctuary and stairs of Nossa Senhora dos Remédios

River Douro

Grape Treading at Quinta do Vesúvio

Grape harvest at Quinta Nova de Nossa Senhora do Carmo

Almond tree in blossom

Quinta do Seixo

Historic train at Pinhão station

River Douro at Régua

With a unique and dazzling landscape, the Upper **Douro** wine region is one of the places considered a World Heritage Site by UNESCO. Many reasons might lead us to this magnificent region, but the most important one is surely the wish to discover the land where the famous wine is produced. This nectar, named Port Wine since the 17th century, grows and matures on the terraces of the many Douro valleys.

Douro was the world's first demarcated and regulated wine region and it is divided into three main regions which differ in geography and climate: Baixo Corgo, Cima Corgo and Upper Douro.

To enjoy the magnificent landscape, you may follow the course of the River Douro by train or on a cruise. During the vintage the several *Quintas* in the region offer you a chance to participate in grape-picking and in the foot treading at the lagares.

Roman Bridge over the River Tâmega

Chaves Castle

Chaves has a unique natural beauty, and several places worth visiting, such as the historical centre, with its Praça Camões. Strongly religious in nature, this municipality offers a large number of churches one should not miss. Other points of interest are, for example, the Roman Bridge; the Região Flaviense Museum; or even the Convent of the Order of Nossa Sra. da Conceição. Widely known are the Chaves Thermal Spa and Vidago Palace Hotel, one of the most luxurious hotels in the country. Gastronomically, note the spicy sausages and the cured meats. The handicraft is also worth mentioning, namely the black pottery, the basketry in Vilar de Nantes and the blankets of Soutelo.

Vidago Palace

Bragança Castle

Bragança is a municipality rich in traditions, and there are plenty of reasons to visit it. Two of the strongest traditions are the *Festas dos Rapazes* and the *Festa dos Caretos* [masks made of wood, leather, tinplate and cork]. The Caretos of Podence, in the municipality of Macedo de Cavaleiros, deserve to be highlighted. These representations of diabolic images go out to the streets, during the carnival festivities, with their cowbells on the colourful fringes of thick blankets.

Bragança is known for its handicraft, a very important activity in the region, and for its gastronomy, whose delicacies must be degusted by all visitors. To those who appreciate natural landscapes, we recommend a visit to the Montesinho Natural Park, which has diverse accommodation, sports and leisure services, perfect for a holiday period in contact with nature. For a longer walk, it is worth visiting the Citadel and all its surroundings, where one can find the *Portas da Vila* (Village Entrance), the castle walls, the Keep, the *Domus Municipalis* and the Pillory.

Domus Municipalis

Caretos de Podence

PUBLICATION:
Objecto Anónimo, Lda.

AUTHOR:
Pedro Rodrigues, Susana Fonseca, Sérgio Fonseca

GRAPHIC DESIGN / PHOTOGRAPHY:
Pedro Rodrigues, Sérgio Fonseca

TEXT EDITING AND COORDINATION:
Susana Fonseca

TEXT COPY:
Susana Fonseca

TRANSLATION:
by Susana Santos. Additional translations and full text revision by Alexandra Andresen Leitão

HISTORIC VALIDATION:
Jorge Pópulo, pages 6, 7, 9, 12, 15, 16, 20, 22 e 24

ACKNOWLEDGEMENTS:
Câmara Municipal do Porto, Instituto dos Vinhos do Douro e Porto, Museu do Douro, Palácio da Bolsa, Igreja de São Francisco, Igreja e Torre dos Clérigos, Sé Catedral do Porto, Casa da Música, Fundação de Serralves, Café Progresso, Café Majestic, Café Ceuta, Café Guarany, Caves Calém, Livraria Lello, Hard Club, Porto Lazer, Futebol Clube do Porto, Teleférico de Gaia - Telef, Terminal de Cruzeiros do Porto e Leixões, Município de Santa Maria da Feira, Palácio da Brejoeira, Casa de Mateus, Quinta da Aveleda, Quinta do Vesúvio, Quinta Nova de Nossa Senhora do Carmo and Palácio de Vidago.

PHOTOGRAPHIC CREDITS:
Departamento de Arquivos da Câmara Municipal do Porto, pages 6 (01), 7, 8 (01)
Coleção do Instituto dos Vinhos do Douro e do Porto, I. P., by Álvaro Cardoso de Azevedo (Casa Alvão), paged 9, 20, 23
Photographs lent by Centro Português de Fotografia:
Alvão Collection, pp. 8, 10 - 11
Panorama do Porto a partir da Serra do Pilar, ALV-032005 | Fachada do Palácio de Cristal, CPF-ALV-004684 |
Caminhos de Ferro do Douro e Minho e Douro - Chegada do 1º comboio à estação do Porto central, CPF-ALV-004676 |
Avenida dos Aliados e Praça da Liberdade com a estátua equestre de D. Pedro IV, CPF-ALV-004718 |
Torre dos Clérigos, CPF-ALV-004688 | Construção da Câmara Municipal do Porto, CPF-ALV-028964;
Museu do Douro, page 21| Futebol Clube do Porto, page 70 (01) | Porto Lazer, page 71 |Vasco Maia Lopes, page 120 (04)
Shutterstock: p. 15 Artur Bogacki, p. 99 (4), p. 99 (1) Marc Venema, p. 107 (1) LuisCostinhaa, p. 121 (1) leoks, p. 122 Csaba Vanyi.

PRINTING:
Norprint - a casa do livro

FIFTH EDITION (revised and updated):
April 2018
1st Edition April 2012
© Objecto Anónimo, Lda.

ALSO AVAILABLE IN THE FOLLOWING LANGUAGES:
Portuguese, French, Spanish and German

COLLECTION JOURNEYS AND STORIES (other publications):
Douro Valley, Lisbon, Portugal, Madeira and Porto Santo

Maia, Portugal
info@objectoanonimo.com

ISBN 978-989-8256-17-1
Depósito Legal 342693/12

Find more books and other products at: